ONE WALLS
DRESSED IN BLACK
GUNS N ROSES
WELCOME TO THE JUNGLE
David Allan Coe Long Haired REDNECK
THE REAPER IS WATCHING YOU!
AIN'T LIFE SO FUCKIN SWEET
REAPER ROWS
SHARING TIME
IF-YOU-DON'T-LIKE HANK WILLIAMS KISS OUR ASS
GUNS N ROSES

Printed in Great Britain
by Amazon

31618665R00018